ILLUMINATIONS

ILLUMINATIONS

Magnifying the Light of Christ through the Pen

Edited by LaTonja Brown

Graphics by Devlin Donnelly

iUniverse LLC
Bloomington

ILLUMINATIONS
Magnifying the Light of Christ through the Pen

iUniverse books may be ordered through booksellers or by contacting:

iUniverse LLC
1663 Liberty Drive
Bloomington, IN 47403
www.iuniverse.com
1-800-Authors (1-800-288-4677)

ISBN: 978-1-4917-0587-2 (sc)
ISBN: 978-1-4917-0589-6 (hc)
ISBN: 978-1-4917-0588-9 (ebk)

Library of Congress Control Number: 2013916006

Printed in the United States of America

iUniverse rev. date: 09/11/2013

Graphics by Devlin Donnelly

Pentecostal Covenant Church
www.site.pentecostalcovenant.org
10033 55th Avenue South, Seattle, WA 98178
(206) 725-7469

Contents

Acknowledgments xi
Introduction xv

Innocence 1
The Prince and the Fairy Princess 3

Loss 7
Kaida: A Story of Puppy Love 9
I Miss My Sister/I Want My Sister Back 14
In Sixty Seconds 17
The Bold Ones, the Hybrids, and the Equipped Ones 19
God Will Perfect It 21

Battle **25**
I Am Armed and Dangerous 27
No Excuses 28
The Last Debate 29
Help Me Build Kingdom Building...31

Illness and Healing...**33**
Drip, Drip 35
Spiritual Remodel 37
The Potter's Hands 39
Spiritual Healing...40
Victory through Transition..42

Faith and Doubt..**45**
Reflections on India..47
Buried Underneath..50
Broken Tears 51

I Know Somebody 52

Hands...53

Jesus Is the Best Way 54

I Had an Audience With the Lord........................55

Only a Few 56

I Am, You Are 57

When God Is in Our Midst.................................58

One Thing I Have Desired..................................59

Relationships and Healing **61**

Forgiveness..63

Dedication to a Chump......................................65

Relationship Freedom 66

Celebrating the Deliverance from Sexual Shame 68

Do You Know? 71

Flights of Fancy...72

Identity and Choice......................................**75**

What's in a Name? 77

Gone Backward...80

Help Me...81

Judge Not...82

I Surrender...83

Dreams..84

A City Called Heaven 86

God Said Live...88

Life or Death..90

Time...**93**

An American Fairytale 95

Where Was God? 96

Time to Begin Again 98

Home Before the Dark.......................................99

Hope..**101**

A Miracle in Haiti..103

Yours to Give 104

Yes, You're the One! 105

Motherhood 107
Songs of Sadness 108
Harlem's Song 110

Contributors 113
About Pentecostal Covenant Church 119
Credits 123

For the writers

Angela, Cheryl, Ursula, and Zarriah

And for You!

This book is dedicated in loving memory
to Mother Cheryl Boyd

*And the LORD answered me, and said, Write the vision, and
make it plain upon tables, so he may run that reads it.*
—Habakkuk 2:2

Empowered by God
To Empower Others

Acknowledgments

First and foremost, thanks to the writers—Angela, Cheryl, Ursula, and Zarriah—who submitted to this anthology! It has been such a pleasure working with you as we learned this process together.

Special thanks to Ursula Lovely, who used her mortality to shame me into getting this project going!

I would like to thank Kris Fulsaas, who has worked with the PCC editors for years now. She has been instrumental in the growth of our editing team and was my editing teacher! She is also the copyeditor for this book!

I would also like to thank Devlin Donnelly who designed the graphics for the anthology. He is so talented in his field not to mention a great coworker!

Thanks to Jo Ann Hairston, Romanita Hairston, and Desiree Prewitt for being my last set of eyes. I am privileged to have such awesome people in my family!

I would also like to thank my friends who have supported my writing over the years and encouraged me to write. You know who you are! You mean more to me than you will ever know.

This anthology would not have been possible without the support of my pastor and first lady, Wilford and Jo Ann Hairston, who are like parents to me. Their love and support has made all of the difference in my life. I love you both so much and words can't do justice to the impact you have had in my life. When nothing else could help, love lifted me!

And, of course, the biggest thank-you goes to God, who gave me a passion and love for words and writing. He saw the project through regardless of my fears, insecurities, procrastination, and best attempts of self-sabotage!

Introduction

I have had a love for words for as long as I can remember, specifically the written word.

As a child, I spent hours with my head in books, and they would take me to another time and another place.

As I began writing, I discovered many things about the written word.

I discovered that writing was extremely healing. It was a place where my thoughts could be organized and sorted out. It was the strangest thing to begin writing and have secrets I was trying to keep from myself suddenly burst into a stream of consciousness so powerful that denial or avoidance was not an option. Knowing the truth, regardless of how painful it was, was the beginning of freedom.

I also discovered that writing was an easy way for me to express myself. When I was little, I had a really bad stutter, especially when I was excited or upset. I was always so conscious of my stutter when I was speaking. But, with writing, I could express myself clearly even when excited or upset. For the most part, my stutter is gone, but writing continues to be the avenue in which I organize my thoughts.

Perhaps the most important discovery I made about writing is that I could create a parallel universe. I could create another time and another place and escape into a safe haven that I created for myself. And these stories did not have to be written down. They could be told in my head when I needed to escape.

As I grew older, my love for words and books continued to grow. To this day, I still love to read, and I still love to write.

Eventually the *PCC Women's Scroll*, now the *PCC Scroll*, came to life; I was surprised by how many writers we had at our church. In the back of mind was the desire to give myself and other writers a platform to publish their works in book form.

And so here we are.

Our youngest submitter is ten years old. Her story is about a princess who finds her prince. Her story is simple and honest and uncomplicated. While I was reading her story, I began to wonder at what age our lives and stories become complicated.

This complication is very clear in the writings of the adult submitters, including myself, whose tone, mood, and emotion move up and down between despair and hope; failure and triumph; and doubt and faith. The writings deal with death, struggle, illness, doubt, broken relationships, identity, abuse, and more.

However, through it all, there is a beacon of light. The human spirit is resilient, and despite the odds, we hold on to our hope and faith. We hold on to our faith that all things work for our good.

These are our words and our stories, and I pray that you will enjoy them.

xoxo
All My Love
LTB

The wolf also shall dwell with the lamb, and the leopard shall lie down with the kid; and the calf and the young lion and the fatling together; and a little child shall lead them.
—Isaiah 11:6

INNOCENCE

The Prince and the Fairy Princess

by Zarriah Polk

Once upon a time, there lived a fairy princess. Her name was Marygold. She was very kind to everyone she saw. She had two sisters. One was sixteen, and one was ten. Marygold was the oldest, at seventeen.

Marygold was so rich that she even had a prince. His name was Charles. He was rich too, but he didn't have any brothers or sisters. He was sad that he did not have any brothers and sisters to look after.

The prince was concerned that he would not get to marry the fairy princess if he did not have a sister. So he pretended that he had a sister. He tried to use one of the princess' sisters, but she knew that it was her sister. So he used his cousin instead. He showed the princess his sister (that was really his cousin), and the princess believed it.

The next day, the prince came to the princess' castle. He knocked on the door. Once inside, he asked the princess to marry him, and the princess said, "Yes!" The prince was very happy that the princess said yes to him.

Two months later, the prince and princess were finally married. She wore a new dress her father got her.

In the end, they had three kids. Their names were Tana, Trania, and Talya.

And they lived happily ever after.

And here is a picture.

And said, Naked came I out of my mother's womb, and naked shall I return there: the LORD gave, and the LORD has taken away; blessed be the name of the LORD.
—Job 1:21

LOSS

Kaida: A Story of Puppy Love

by Ursula Lovely

This is a story that began in the year 2004. It is a story of puppy love that will last forever more. Two young people, who decided to become husband and wife, made a decision together as they began a new life.

Oh, who am I, you might ask? I am the mother of the bride, and I am privy to the story from the inside.

The couple, Pamela and Martez, decided that they wanted to purchase a puppy. They wanted to get a Tosa Inu mastiff. What I didn't know was that this particular breed would grow to be so massive. They began their search for breeders and even on the internet far and wide. Would you believe that on their way to the gym one day in a yard nearby the pup was spied? They felt she was the cutest and most perfect dog they had ever seen, but they had to wait a little while for her to be weaned.

It is funny as I look back on it. For all intents and purposes, Kaida was their first baby. She was good training for them because of the things puppies and babies have in common. Puppies and babies need to be taken care of. They both slobber a lot, and both, in a way, have to be taught to use the pot. Now, it wasn't a surprise to the kids how much Kaida grew. The size of this pup was something that they always knew.

At the beginning of the story, my husband and I had moved to Arizona for a while. Then we received a cute little bear in the mail that informed us that the couple was now with child. When we got over the shock and the excitement settled in, we couldn't wait. We sold everything that was not nailed down and headed back to Washington State.

On December 2, 2006, a new chapter of the story begins. That is when Makaila was born and Kaida got a new friend. I remember after the baby was born, we took a receiving blanket in which Makaila was held, so that Kaida could sleep with it and get accustomed to the baby's smell. When we finally brought the baby home, we let Kaida smell her and kiss her little face. After this was done, it was like Kaida said, "Okay, she's all right. She can stay in this place."

They grew together for seven months or more. During this time, Makaila was poking eyes and pulling ears, and one day we placed Makaila on the floor. Can you imagine what Kaida was thinking as the baby started to crawl her way? Maybe something like, "Who told you guys that I was ready to play?" Makaila had a determined look upon her face, a look like, "This will be fun." Kaida saw her coming and turned and immediately started to run. Makaila was small but never frail. The only problem that she had was with Kaida bumping her and wagging and hitting her with her tail.

Picture this: Kaida sitting in an open back door. Makaila crawls to the door and seems to be asking her, "Okay, what are we waiting for? Let's go." We thought it was bad for poor Kaida when Makaila learned to walk. We had no idea what the puppy would be in for when the baby started to talk. Makaila would take Kaida's toys and run as a tease. Kaida couldn't ask her to please give it back. The only way she could communicate was to growl. That's the way she could get through. Makaila would look at her and say, "Kaida, stop it. Nobody's afraid of you."

Then there was the time Uncle Craig gave Makaila a toy truck to ride. You guessed it. Makaila chased poor Kaida, who could only run and search for a place to hide. Makaila was never afraid of this dog that was four times her size. Kaida would give in to her commands and just step aside. When Makaila was just two years old, she would walk Kaida outside on a leash, and Kaida would obey and do as she was told. This odd pair had a friendship that was good as gold. Kaida was such a good dog, and she loved the family so. She would protect them at home and wherever they would go.

In 2010, two things happened, one good and one that was bad. The good thing was a beautiful baby, a little sister, McKenna, joined the family. And then the news that was sad. Kaida had begun to lose weight and be less active. The young couple took her to the vet to get an answer. The news was not good. We learned that Kaida had cancer. They told Makaila that Kaida was ill and going to die. The only question she had for them was, "Why?"

They watched Kaida carefully for any serious signs she would show. A week before Kaida died, Makaila informed her parents that she didn't want Kaida to go.

It was a Sunday morning, and we were at church when my daughter and son-in-law brought Kaida to say goodbye. It was a sad morning, and all of us had tears in our eyes. I am just so glad that Makaila had been prepared because on February 13, 2011, Kaida, a part of our family and our friend, went to be with God in heaven.

Footnote: The other day, Makaila told her mother that God could send Kaida back now.

I Miss My Sister/
I Want My Sister Back

by LaTonja Brown

Mid-September to early October is a hard time for me.

September 21 is my sister Honey's birthday. She died in a car accident when I was twenty-three, in other words, sixteen years ago.

The last conversation I had with her was in mid-September. She called to talk to me, but I was too tired to talk. I remember us laughing as I was trying to hang up, but she wanted to talk. I was like, "Dude, I have to go," and practically hung up on her. She tried calling back, but I did not pick up the phone. She urgently wanted to talk to me.

Fast-forward about a week to her twenty-fifth birthday, and I could not reach her. I tried and I tried but just couldn't connect. I was not able to wish her a happy birthday. I urgently wanted to talk to her.

Fast-forward a few weeks to the call I never wanted to get.

My sister knew/knows I love her. But that final conversation we had when I did not tell her one last time will always stay with me. That final conversation when I was too tired to take the time to talk to her will always stay with me.

Now I try to hug my friends and family when I see them. I try to tell them that I love them because you never really know when it will be the last time.

Her death taught me a lot about who actually cared for me. I remember I sought out comfort from people who I thought would comfort me, but you know how that goes.

I went through a lot of guilt over her dying and not me. She had kids; I had none. I kept asking God why (and I still haven't gotten an answer to that question). I was so angry when she died. I remember when I turned twenty-five; I didn't feel like I had the right to turn that age. Then I turned twenty-six, and so on, and so on.

I remember sitting at her funeral stone-faced and mad at the world. The only person I was not mad at was our sister, Cathy.

I still haven't cried about it. I just suppress the emotion, like if I cry it will be admitting that she is gone from this life. It's like the last picture I have with her. That's it.

The funny thing is that I still expect to pick up the phone and hear her voice. She still owes me money. She used to make me laugh. She could have been a comedian. I am thankful for the time we had as sisters, and what a time it was.

- I remember Cathy, Honey, and I singing "We Are Family" with towels on our heads when we were little.
- I remember Cathy, Honey, and I staying up every Christmas Eve and watching *A Christmas Story* all night.
- I remember Cathy, Honey, and I staying up watching *Night Tracks* on Fridays and Saturdays.
- I remember Cathy, Honey, and I staying up all night the night before the first day of school each year.
- I remember Cathy, Honey, and I doing our first solo plane trip together.
- I remember Cathy, Honey, and I being in Jump Rope for Heart together.
- I remember Cathy, Honey, and I playing house and dolls together. I also remember early on when LaQuita, our cousin, would play with us. LaQuita was Big Tina, Cathy

was Judy. I forgot Honey's name, but I was CeCe, and I hated that name.

- I remember Cathy, Honey, and I used to go trick-or-treating, and we would go far from home.
- I remember Cathy, Honey, and I working in our aunt's garden like slaves. We were so bitter to be out there.
- I remember Cathy, Honey, and I picking plums from this tree in Moses Lake.
- I remember the time Honey got stung by a bee and swelled like a balloon and had to be taken to the hospital. We didn't realize it was actually life threatening and laughed and laughed and laughed. Actually, it's still funny.
- I remember Honey was allergic to everything and had asthma.
- I remember Honey teaching me how to fight.
- I remember one night at dinner Honey didn't want to eat what was on her plate. Our aunt made her sit there, and then she started crying because she said a spider was following her. That was hilarious!
- I remember when Honey made some rolls from a recipe she learned in home economics, and they were harder than rocks.
- I remember Honey coming to visit me when I was at the UW.
- I remember Honey doing my hair when I was a teenager.
- I remember when I was in sixth grade, I used to wear my sisters' clothes without them knowing it. They left for school before me, and I got back before them. I would wear their stuff and then rush home and put it back in their closets.
- I remember that it's good to remember.

In Sixty Seconds

by Ursula Lovely

I have no major desire to fill you with fear,
But do you realize that in sixty seconds every earthly
Thing that you value could just disappear.

I understand the need to get all we can.
That seems to be in the nature of man.

Be assured that measure of a man is not his worth.
What people truly remember him for is the love he gets
And gives while he is on this earth.

As we mature,
Life sometimes seems like a never-ending night
With little or no hope of ever reaching the light.

Is there someone you intended to call today?
Is there something you meant to say,
But somehow forgot to say?

Don't keep putting off things until tomorrow
Because if you wait the only thing that may come is sorrow.

Reach out and express your love
To family and to the Lord above.

In these past few months,
Have we not seen the things people have gathered around
Destroyed and turned into nothing but empty ground?

Treasure the people around you and
The God you must reckon
Because what we know today is that everything can be gone in
    just sixty seconds.

The Bold Ones, the Hybrids, and the Equipped Ones

by Angela Davis

My cousin, Karryl Yvette, died December 2011 at the age of forty-four. I can't believe she is gone, but the fact of the matter is that we are all going to die. During the death of a loved one, we try to reconcile internally whether we will go to heaven or hell. Do we live to die, or do we die to live?

During the repast after her service, I saw so many contrasts and contradictions. It is amazing how, through a spiritual eye, dark, muted hues and bright, exhilarating hues are illuminated through the bodies of those at this repast. The contrasts and contradictions can be metaphorically explained as stages of spiritual awareness. They can be described by three spiritual stages that I have named the Bold Ones, the Hybrids, and the Equipped Ones.

The Bold Ones were genuine for Satan regardless of the situations in their lives. They were drinking and cursing up a storm. I must hand it to them; they were wholehearted in what they did and who they represented even if they don't have the awareness of doing so.

The Hybrids talked about the Lord and accepted Him in their lives but drank, smoked, and cursed. Accepting and acknowledging that Jesus is the King of kings and Lord of lords ignites an eternal transition that creates growth—naturally, emotionally, and spiritually, which is crucial during the loss of a loved one.

The Equipped Ones were the individuals representing Jesus Christ to the best of their human abilities. They regularly witness, pray continuously, and love beyond natural comprehension. They are dedicated to God and use their vessels for the Lord. During the repast, the Equipped Ones saw, heard, and prayed while sitting stoically in their chairs. They responded outwardly only by the prompting of the Holy Spirit, and that was amazing in itself, based on the many forms of human interaction that occurred that day.

These three "types" were harmoniously in the same house. But there was a forceful battle raging that was audible to the spiritual ear and visible with the spiritual eye but not visible to the natural ear and eye. I do not judge anyone because we determine our outcomes by our choices. Choices cannot be rationally decided if you do not have adequate information. Similarly, in the spiritual realm, we cannot be the Equipped Ones until we become completely dedicated. Even the Equipped Ones are in the same transitional process of dying daily as the Bold Ones and the Hybrids.

There becomes a realization that, as long as we are in these earthly vessels, there are no individuals who have "arrived." God has no big I's or little you's. Christians just choose to be used by God with the ultimate goal, through our passion and love of God, to become a witness for Him through our lives. I process the sorrow of losing my cousin with the hope that we will all meet again. We must transition from the Bold Ones to the Hybrids, and finally to the Equipped Ones.

I pray, as time brings about many changes, that our family becomes an army of equipped soldiers—hearing and marching to the audible voice of the Holy One, the lover of my soul, Jesus Christ.

In loving memory of my "cuz" Karryl Yevette Smith, who loved big, smiled widely, and died too soon.

God Will Perfect It

By LaTonja Brown

There has been a lot of death in the last several months.

On May 1, the pastor of the church I attended when I was a child passed away. I was able to reconnect with him and his wife a few years ago and thank them for all they did for me and my sisters when we were growing up.

On May 14, my grandmother on my dad's side passed away. Although I didn't know her that well, it was sad to hear of her passing. She was my last living grandparent.

On June 7, the aunt of one of my close friends passed away. I spent two and a half weeks with my friend's aunt during my trip to India. She was such a strong woman, a historian, and a storyteller. She and the other ladies I stayed with found a sacred place in my heart.

June 3 was the one-year anniversary of the passing of my aunt who raised me. As the day grew closer, I felt the same raw emotion arise in me that I feel each year at the anniversary of my sister's death. My subconscious becomes sad and tender, and then the date hits me like a ton of bricks. I remember all the things I didn't say and all the things I didn't do with a deep regret, but I can't change the past.

Death brings about questions and thoughts about my own mortality. What will I accomplish before my appointed time in this life ends? There are things I want to do. There is the ever-growing list of places I want to travel to. I also want to write a novel. But what do I need to accomplish that is for God that will last? What is my legacy? What is my assignment? What is my function in the body of Christ?

I am inspired by the accomplishments of my friends. My friend Toyia completed her master's degree and is working toward establishing a school in the Seattle area. My friend Samarah is holding a summer program for women of color in the L.A. area that is focused on college preparation and entrepreneurial training. As their dreams begin to unfold and take shape, I am motivated to fulfill my own destiny.

I am drawn to Psalm 138:8, which reads, *"The LORD will perfect that which concerneth me: thy mercy, O LORD, endureth for ever: forsake not the works of thine own hands."*

I am so glad that God has not forgotten His desire for any of us. He has given each of us another day to fulfill our destiny and calling in Him. God will bring us to a place where we can achieve what He desires of us. There is an appointed time, and it will come to pass!

I am so looking forward to being inspired by *your* accomplishments. I will leave you with Philippians 1:6, which says, *"Being confident of this very thing, that he which hath begun a good work in you will perform it until the day of Jesus Christ."*

Wherefore take unto you the whole armour of God, that ye may be able to withstand in the evil day, and having done all, to stand.
Stand therefore, having your loins girt about with truth, and having on the breastplate of righteousness; And your feet shod with the preparation of the gospel of peace; Above all, taking the shield of faith, wherewith ye shall be able to quench all the fiery darts of the wicked. And take the helmet of salvation, and the sword of the Spirit, which is the word of God.
—Ephesians 6:13-17

BATTLE

I Am Armed and Dangerous

by Cheryl Boyd

I'm armed and dangerous
And on a mission for the Lord.
I'm wearing the Helmet of salvation
And know the Word is sharper than any two-edged sword.
I'm armed and dangerous, devil.
You can't stop me now.
I've got the right ammunition,
And I'll use it like my God taught me how.
I'm armed and dangerous with Jesus on my side.
I won't run from you, devil, and I refuse to hide.

I'm armed and dangerous, devil.
I'm going to kick you to the curb
Because you need to know you've gotten on my last nerve.

I'm armed and dangerous, Satan.
Disturb my house? No you don't.
You've got to get to stepping. Defeat me? Oh, no you won't.

I'm armed and dangerous, devil.
I'm going to stomp you to the ground.
For you see, I've been with the Lord
And felt His presence all around.

I'm armed and dangerous, Satan.
You'd better get out of my way.
I'm armed and dangerous
And that's how I'm going to stay.

No Excuses

by Ursula Lovely

Excuses are how we play this life game.
It's what we use to shift the blame.
Like, "I don't know why. I guess the devil made me do it."
Instead of just admitting that we blew it.

Or, "I guess I had too much to drink."
Whose decision was it to take the first one, do you think?
If you are really trying to save your soul,
Don't you think asking God and some work from you could
Give you some control?

Stand up tall and beat your chest
Like you do when you have done your best.
Admit to the Lord that the only one to blame is you,
That you did what you wanted to do.

Now, pick an army like you did as a child that will help you to win.
Choose to do the right things and fight against sin.
Remember that you are the one who can choose,
That this game is yours to win or lose.

This is something that we must do every day,
One that is hard and never seems to go away.
The goal is worth it as we go forward.
The prize is an everlasting spiritual life with the Lord.

The Last Debate

by LaTonja Brown

Toward the end of the movie version of *Lord of the Rings: Return of the King*, there is a Last Debate. The Debate is whether hundreds of Men should engage in battle against thousands of Orcs. During this scene, the dwarf Gimli makes a statement along the lines that they will certainly die and they have a small probability of achieving success. He then goes on to ask what they are waiting for.

I absolutely *love* this line, but if these were my marching orders, would I engage in battle?

I barely engage in a war where I know the outcome.

With my intellect, I realize there is a "fixed" war. I already know the outcome. God will have victory. I piggyback God's victory and proclaim I will have victory. It makes me happy. It makes me gleeful. It makes me gloat. It makes me lazy.

It makes me lazy?

I am very guilty of taking advantage of this known victory. The main reason is lack of wisdom in processing the significance of this victory.

I have the victory. I am in a "fixed" war. Why do I need to train? Why do I need to condition? In my bedridden state, I can stay under the covers. I can mope. I can withdraw. I can take for granted that God will step in and rescue me. I can have the victory?

I have thoughts like how do I really know what side I am on? How can I be sure? What are the signs that I actually know Him versus know *of* Him?

I think I am beginning to understand better. This knowledge should not make us lazy. This knowledge should not validate willingly losing a battle here and there because of a won war. This knowledge should propel us into battle. We should confidently engage in war against our enemy because we know that no weapon formed against us will prosper. We must prepare ourselves for battle. Read Ephesians 6:11-18.

In *Return of the King*, victory could not be achieved by strength of arms. Our victory will never be achieved by strength of arms either—at least not physical strength of arms. "*This is the word of the LORD . . . Not by might, nor by power, but by my spirit, saith the LORD of hosts.*"

I invite us all to engage in this battle. In truth, whether we choose to engage in battle or not, the war is coming to us. The plan to attack your life is in place, and the units are moving toward you.

Our temptations are coming, but they won't come from the paths we suspect or are used to. The temptations are coming, and now is not the time to flirt with them.

What are the marching orders for our battle?

Certainty of (everlasting) life, huge chance of success . . . what're we waiting for?

Help Me Build Kingdom Building

by Cheryl Boyd

Help me build kingdom building
By praying, fasting, testimony, and songs of praise.
Help me build kingdom building
Here in the house of Grace.

By knocking on doors and passing out tracts,
Help me build kingdom building
According to the second chapter of Acts.

Through the Men's and Women's Groups,
Youth and Pastor's Aid too.
Help me build kingdom building
By teaching and adding to our Sunday school.

By giving self and money cheerfully
And loving each man, woman, girl, and boy.
Help me build kingdom building
And hear heaven's bells ring for you.

It does not matter what your gifts may be,
Whether it's song, healing, or exhortation.
Help me build kingdom building,
And this you will agree:
That there is a greater building
On high for you and for me!

But he was *wounded for our transgressions, he* was *bruised for our iniquities: the chastisement of our peace* was *upon him; and with his stripes we are healed.*
—Isaiah 53:5

ILLNESS AND HEALING

Drip, Drip

by Angela Davis

Today was my second chemotherapy treatment. I dread the physical side effects of nausea, diarrhea, fatigue, and the enormous appetite induced by a steroid called prednisone, but I look forward to telling the report that I am healed *and* whole. I feel so blessed to know that so many people are supporting me, and I know that God will take care of all of my needs.

It was a blessing that my Aunt Eleanor was able to spend a large amount of time with me. She took the bus and the trolley and then walked up the steep hill to the Seattle Cancer Care Alliance. She really liked the doctor, Dr. Andrei Shustov, and was impressed with the aesthetic of the building.

Chemotherapy is administered intravenously and is designed to kill the cells that hinder the normal functioning of the human body. Similarly, the Holy Spirit is designed to transform our hearts from the sinful nature to the yielding of His grace and mercy.

I pray, as the minute particles that are infused into my body to rid itself of the tumor, that God will go into the minute areas of my brokenness and mend me completely so I can effectively do His will. I pray that I will have the holy boldness to obey His instructions and complete what He ordained me to do.

I believe that when we ask God for things with sincerity and the right motives, He will honor those requests. The important thing is to be honest and open and have consistent communication with God. I claim wholeness through the power of the Holy Spirit. The cleansing of my natural body is for temporary gain, but the spiritual cleansing is for eternal gain. The flow of the Living

Water is free and limitless. The flow of the man-made water is limited. Both forms of liquid substances are crucial in my case, chemotherapy for natural life and Living Water for eternal life.

I have accepted the process of pain and healing, sadness and joy. As these tears drip I say, "Let everything that needs to flow in my life drip. Let them drip . . ."

Spiritual Remodel

by LaTonja Brown

I'm currently remodeling my condominium. For over a month, I have been living out of boxes. My life seems extremely chaotic right now. I was bemoaning my current existence when it occurred to me how long I comfortably lived in spiritual and mental disorder and chaos.

I began musing on spiritual remodeling. When we accept Christ in our life, we become a new creation, and we are in a constant state of "remodeling."

During this adventure, I have learned that there are standard items that can be bought directly from the store because they fit most homes. Then there are items that are unique to my home. These customized items need to be specially ordered, which takes longer.

I began the project by seeking wise counsel, like Esther sought the counsel of Mordecai. I sought the counsel of those who knew about remodeling a home. The next step was to work on the timing or schedule for each project. I knew painting would be messy. It seemed like the logical place to start. If my carpet was replaced before painting, I would end up blemishing my new wood floors.

Painting was easy enough. Although my walls were dirty, I didn't have to clean them before painting them. When I applied paint to the wall, all trace of the dirt was gone. The paint covered my walls in the meaning of the Hebrew word *kaphar*. This means "to cover, appease, pacify, pardon, reconcile, cancel, purge away." The word *kaphar* translates as "make atonement."

The other projects will be harder. My dirty old carpet will need to be ripped up. Not only is this physically demanding, but there are tasks that need to be completed before the carpet can be removed.

I had to pack all my books and belongings to make them mobile. It was a step I couldn't get around. During this process, I took the time to really go through my belongings. I was able to purge items that no longer fit my personal style for today and would not fit in my new remodeled home.

In the course of taking an inventory of my life, I found some items I thought I had lost. Some things had dropped between the cracks. Other items had just been filed in the wrong place. Other items I no longer needed, but I had not brought myself to let them go. Other items I had just put away and never dealt with. This exercise served as a good method to do away with the old and make room for the new. Because I have a new color scheme, some of my old things just don't match anymore.

The project is at the point where I can visually picture the finished result, and it looks good! The energy and resources that are being exerted will increase the value of my home. Each step brings out more and more of the potential that was always there.

There are times when I wish I could picture myself as the finished project God has imagined, but perhaps I would spend so much time admiring the finished picture that I wouldn't do the work to bring it from the spiritual into the natural.

None of us are finished projects. We are all uniquely designed, and God has customized specifications for our blueprints. This season is a time when the vision for my life is becoming clearer.

I look forward to watching the potential in each of us emerge as we are being spiritually remodeled.

The Potter's Hands

by Cheryl Boyd

I may be sick.
I may be well.
But I've got something to the world to tell.
I'm being made perfect day and night.
The Lord Himself made my crooked ways right.
The devil may think he's got me on the run,
But I'm saved by the grace of God's only Son.
I put my life in the Potter's hands,
And with the Lord I'll make my stand.
The Potter's Hands are molding me with loving care.
It has nothing to do with my clothes or the way I wear my hair.
Living for Jesus is my only goal.
Jesus is the Potter, and I am the clay.
I'm giving notice to the devil that I'm going to stay.

Spiritual Healing

by LaTonja Brown

At the end of September, I had surgery to remove fibroids. I asked my mother to come and be with me as I recovered. My mother did not raise me, and our relationship has been pretty up and down over the course of my life. I thought it would be an opportunity for us to relate as mother and daughter.

My mother's not raising me had a profound impact on my life and deeply impacted my feelings of self-worth. In short, I suffered from feelings of abandonment and rejection. When I was younger, I used to have an internal dialogue about my being unlovable. My mother's not wanting or loving me was the only proof that I needed. During those conversations, another voice would enter that simply said, "God loves you."

Even though I knew God's love was the end-all, I spent years looking for love. I desperately sought this seemingly elusive word called love. My friend Billie Washington once told me that God was going to send me love. I remember her pivotal words made me cry. God has sent me love. "Pressed down, and shaken together, and running over" love. I'm loved to the point that I'm spoiled, which is okay (smile and laugh).

During the time with my mom, I discovered that my mom does love me. Her visit ended up being a wonderful family reunion. I was reunited with cousins who live in the Seattle area whom I had not seen or talked to in *years*. I was reunited with the aunt who raised me whom I had not seen or talked to in *years*. I discovered that my family does love me. It was a great experience, and my family underwent healing. I parallel the recovery I went through after surgery with the recovery that is happening within my family.

Over the years, I had something growing inside of me naturally that I didn't even know was there. It was only when the growth got so uncomfortable that I couldn't ignore the impact that it had on my life that I took action. I learned that the fibroids were located in a place where they could block conception when it was time for me to try to have a child. If I had gotten pregnant, there would have been complications because the baby would have been unable to grow properly.

In the same way, the bitterness and anger I felt toward my family was blocking the spiritual gifts that God would have me birth. Both issues, natural and spiritual, needed the hands of a trained surgeon to remove what was blocking conception and hindering a safe place for a gift to grow.

What does God need to surgically remove from you? Life is too short to hold onto grudges and to hold onto past offenses. The Master Surgeon is ready to perform a surgery of miracles on you. The Church is filled with trained nurses and staff to assist with the surgery and shower you with love and attention as you recover.

Victory through Transition

by Cheryl Boyd

My body may be wracked
With pain,
But by and by
New strength I gain.

I raise my hands toward
God and praise His name for all
Victory through transition.

I may have lost my job
And feel like I've just been robbed;
"Please help me, Lord,"
I eventually sob for
Victory through transition.

I've just laid a precious loved
One to rest;
Contain my heartache,
I'll do my best.

I feel the Lord's
Gentle hands on my heart,
Giving me
Victory through my transition.

I won't weep
And I won't mourn.
I refuse to act
Or even feel down.

Though my life seems
Battered and torn,
My God gives
Victory through my transition.

Jesus said, "I'm the way, the truth, and the life.
I alone will guide you every night and day."
By my side, that's where He will stay,
Constantly giving me
Victory through my transition.

*Yea, though I walk through the valley of the shadow of death, I
will fear no evil: for thou art with me; thy rod
and thy staff they comfort me.*
—Psalm 23:4

FAITH AND
DOUBT

Reflections on India

by LaTonja Brown

I feel as if I am going to implode at any second.

I went to India for a month this summer for vacation.

I saw beautiful monuments like the Taj Mahal. I saw beautiful countryside in the north and the south. I ate delicious food. I met wonderful people.

I saw some not so good things. My heart hurt when I saw kids working in fields when they should have been in school. I was deeply disturbed to see families living in tents with no electricity or running water.

While I was there, I was praying, hoping, and waiting for a deep revelation about life. It never came.

While I was there, I was waiting for God "to come and get me." In order to fully understand and appreciate this statement, you needed to have been at a past leadership training on Sunday morning. He didn't come.

Then I came back to Seattle. I went from the mountaintop to some deep valley.

Since I've been back, I've been a little down. In truth, I've been a lot down. I know, I know; saints of the highest God should never be down. Jeremiah lamented. I lament.

I've been asked by coworkers and friends for pictures and stories. I haven't felt like sharing anything. In truth, I haven't felt like engaging back into normal life. My only high point since being back in the United States was a trip to Los Angeles during Labor Day weekend. It would appear that the minute I enter work or church, I close in.

Since I'm one to fester, I've been thinking about how I feel. I haven't taken any steps to stop feeling this way. I am just thinking about it. I'm wondering why I feel this way. Is this normal?

When I was in India, I felt like I was a stranger in a strange land. Now that I'm home, I feel like I'm a stranger in a strange land.

Have I been traumatized by the trip? Perhaps. I can't identify any particular "event" though.

I have been drawn to the story of Joseph. Is there a life lesson lurking in the story? I've been thinking and searching for parallels. Nothing.

It would appear that I'm having a hard time placing the person who returned from India in the life of the person who left for India.

When I was in India, I was the person with affluence. I never did adjust to that. When I was in India, it was best to not engage with women and children asking for money. A more direct translation would be, it was better to ignore them. In my need to be seen, it was heartbreaking to not see people.

I kept thinking about justice. I kept thinking about grace. I kept thinking about mercy. Who am I, that I was born in a developed country? Who am I, that I was able to attend a university? Who am I, that I have a decent job with a decent home?

For $160, I can pay for a child's tuition, uniform, and text books in India. What will I do with this information?

If salvation is the Word becoming Flesh and dwelling among people, how does that happen?

How does one pass through feelings of inadequacy and self-doubt and make an impact?

How does light shine through darkness? How does peace give rest? How does love give light?

When faced with great injustice and evil, what will I do?

When I was in India, I had questions without answers. Now I still have no answers; I only have more questions. Everything, it seems, is in direct contradiction. I think I'm okay with that.

Buried Underneath

by Ursula Lovely

Going through the clutter of my mind,
Do you know what I happened to find?

Underneath words heard for years,
Covered with pain and tears,

Like in an attic in an old trunk,
Under years of negative junk,

Something that's been there all the while,
Words I heard somewhere as a child,

Over here under, "Isn't there anything right you can do?"
Hidden were the words "Yes, Jesus Loves You!"

Broken Tears

by Cheryl Boyd

I was sinking in sin and despair,
Thinking that no one for me did care.
I cried and cried and asked the Lord, "Why me?"
I was in a tunnel and no light could I see.
I pleaded to God, "If you are whom people say,
I need you in my life today."
I did something that I hadn't done in years.
I communed with the LORD and in my eyes were broken tears.
These tears that were shed were of anger, pain, and strife
From all the torment I suffered in my life.
As I began to read the Word,
For the first time in my life, I felt the true presence of the Lord.
He wrapped His strong arms around me, and He rocked me
    in His love.
Oh, that wonderful feeling given to me that was so sweet from
    above.
He gave me strength to endure, peace, and joy sublime.
I realized what I'd been missing in life for the very first time.
I thanked and praised God for taking away my pain and fears.
And yes, for fixing those broken-hearted tears.

I Know Somebody

by Cheryl Boyd

I know somebody
Who can give you peace of mind.
I know somebody
Who can give you joy sublime.
I know somebody
Who can put a song in your heart.
I know somebody
Who loves from the start.
I know somebody
Who healed the sick and caused blind eyes to see.
His Name is Jesus.
He's waiting to do the same for you and me.
I know somebody
Who's the way, the truth, and the life.
We say get down on your knees
With a surrendered heart and lift up your voice and pray.
Jesus will lead, guide, and direct in the way that you go
If you only allow Him.
His wondrous blessings on you will ever flow.
I know somebody.

Hands

by Cheryl Boyd

Hands that caused the blind to see
Are the same hands that beckoned
"Come to me."

Hands that comforted the poor
And healed the sick where they lay
Belonged to the man whom Judas did betray.

Hands that raised the dead from the grave
Are the same hands for salvation
He gave.

Hands that bled on Calvary's cross for us
Are owned by the man whose name is Jesus!

Jesus Is the Best Way

by Cheryl Boyd

His way is the best
Every hour of every day.
His way is the best.
Let this be my goal, I pray.

For He saved me from a world of sin
And gave me wonderful peace and joy within.
This is why I smile and say,
Jesus is the best!

I Had an Audience With the Lord

by Cheryl Boyd

I had an Audience with the Lord, and it was so sweet.
I was able to touch His robe and sit at His feet.

He told me He loved me and keeps me in His care.
But I must read my word and go to Him in earnest prayer.

I had an Audience with the Lord, although things were going
   wrong.
My pockets were empty, but in my heart, I still had a praise and
   song.

I was in bed in pain like I'd never felt before,
But I opened up my ears and my Lord was knocking at my door.

I summoned Him to come in and bade the Lord to stay awhile.
As Jesus and I communed, I know this cramped the devil's style.

The devil was made as mad as could be,
For he knew that at that moment I'd won the victory!

The Bible says to resist the devil, and he will flee from you.
But this can only happen with Jesus in your life all the way
   through.

I had an Audience with the Lord, and He made everything all
   right.
You too can have that same audience, and it matters not if it be day
   or night.

I had an Audience with the Lord.

Only a Few

by Cheryl Boyd

Only a few
Were at my Savior's side.
Only a few
Went where He did abide.

Although He healed and taught people plenty,
On that sad day—a friend He had not any.

Only a few
Heeded to His call.
Only a few
Yielded their all in all.

Dare I be among the chosen few?
This is my daily prayer,
When my time is due.
Only a few.

I Am, You Are

by Ursula Lovely

There is one thing we need to understand.
We did not create God. God made man.

We must begin to get our priorities straight,
Hear His Word before it is too late.

After all these years the joke is on us, and it is not funny.
You see, the riches that we seek have absolutely nothing to do with
    money.

We were given these physical bodies that we have been trying to
    please since birth,
When in reality what we are seeking will come after this earth.

I have no idea why we have made it this far,
But now I understand that I am, Dear Lord, because You are!

When God Is in Our Midst

by Cheryl Boyd

The beauty of holiness does dispel
When God is in our midst.
Trouble and heartache disappear
When God is in our midst.
His peace and joy are so near
When God is in our midst.
His presence is so divine
When God is in our midst.
His love is forever yours and mine
When God is in our midst.

One Thing I Have Desired

by Cheryl Boyd

Just a little closer walk with the Lord.
I desire a greater understanding of your Word.
I desire to sup and converse with you more.
I'm tired of all this trouble and life's war.
But, Lord, I desire to walk closer to thee.
One thing have I desired, Lord,
And it is to be your precious child.
Also to hear your voice so tender and mild.
I want you to hold me in your loving arms,
Keeping me safe from danger and harm.
No good things will He withhold from you
If we desire to seek the Lord from now until eternity.
You will live your life with complete victory.
One thing have I desired of the Lord is to feel His anointing
    from above.
Without His anointing, I wouldn't know the power of God's love.
I want to enjoy the full Holy Ghost in its full power and might,
For we need it every day and every hour.
I love the Lord, and I know He loves you too.

For if ye forgive men their trespasses,
your heavenly Father will also forgive you.
—Matthew 6:14

RELATIONSHIPS AND HEALING

Forgiveness

by LaTonja Brown

Forgiveness is not a choice.

In some ways, it pains me to say that. There are people who have hurt me so bad that I feel I have the right to hate them with a perfect hatred. I feel I am justified for the anger and the bitterness I feel toward them. The grudge I have toward them is like the Energizer bunny; it keeps going and going.

Forgiveness is a commandment.

I was listening to the radio on the way home from Bible Study one Wednesday. The topic was forgiveness. The guest speaker said he reads the following scripture every morning: "*Judge not, and ye shall not be judged; condemn not, and ye shall not be condemned; forgive, and ye shall be forgiven.*"

We can't pick and choose whom we decide to forgive. Not forgiving whatever my aunt, mom, dad, Johnnie, Susie, ___ did is not worth losing my mind or salvation.

It's been a year (or two or three), but I'm still bitter. Meanwhile, the other person has moved on. Meanwhile, the bitterness is causing stress in my relationships with other people. It's causing stress in my body.

I firmly believe that some physical illnesses are manifestations of internal conflict. The devil is a liar. My right to be angry, bitter, and disillusioned is not worth my health. Women tend to let fools—and let's face it, the dude was a fool—hurt them to the point where they don't trust other people. This lack of trust damages all relationships you have with those around you. Your anger is misdirected toward innocent people.

I would like to encourage you to think about people you know you have issues and beef with. Once you determine that, for your own sake, do whatever you need to do to let it go and move on. Write them a letter, which you don't have to send. Talk to them about it. Talk to God about it. Ask Him to help you release that person. Stop focusing on the past and look to the future. What is your divine destiny? Can you really reach it if you are hung up on the issues of the past?

When we refuse to forgive someone, we also tend to sit in judgment of that person. For me, I have cursed and condemned people because of my self-righteousness (pray for me, please). We will all reap what we sow. If that person needs to be thumped on the head, let God do it. Whatever God does is better than anything we could think, do, or say.

Are any of us that perfect that we can condemn and judge people?

Forgiveness not being a choice also frees me. It frees me to forgive myself. It frees me to say that most people who hurt me did not do it intentionally. They may have been acting out of their own hurt or immaturity—people who are hurting hurt other people. They may have been doing the best they could with what they had. Or, like me, they could hurt others out of an unhealthy self-defense mechanism.

Whatever the reason, open your hand and let go of the past. Open up your heart and mind to the future. Don't hold people a prisoner to their past (there go I but by the Grace of God). I know I don't want to be held a prisoner to mine.

Lord, help me to love with a perfect love.

Dedication to a Chump

by Angela Davis

During the cycle of life, the truth about a person will eventually come out. The sweet-talking, fun-loving times with a person can be very deceiving. Being caught up in an aura of happiness eventually dissipates. Because of that realization, I have chosen to write this dedication.

My, how I would like to slice you up into deli slices and serve you at your wife's front door. But, praise the Lord. The fact of the matter is that God has enough compassion to let you see another day. Because of this fact, I must acknowledge that your life means something. That is why I will simply thank you for the memories, you lying, cheating, and slimy chump.

I have learned, thanks to you, to never let a low-life man destroy my sanity, dreams, and dignity. But, most of all, I refuse to allow your deceitfulness to cause the fall of my faith in God. He is the same yesterday, today, and forever.

Because of His grace, repentance is sufficient to deal with my heart and actions. I have gained another understanding of His grace; I will leave you in His hands. The pain you have caused will go away as the sin we both allowed to go on.

So this is the dedication I leave to you: May God deal with you as you continue on your day. God knows that if it wasn't for His grace, you would not be breathing nor have the capability to read this dedication to you.

Relationship Freedom

by LaTonja Brown

My aunt who raised me died in early June. Death brings many questions about the health of a relationship. Did I visit enough? Did I call enough? What was our last conversation? Did I make time for her, or did I rush her off of the phone? Did I tell her I loved her?

Relationships are like gardens. They must be nourished, watered, and groomed. If not, they will be forgotten and abandoned and will grow wild. A week will become a month. A month will become a year. Weeds will consume the relationship and suck it dry. In the end, the root of the issues that caused the problems become so entangled and intertwined that they are hard to sort out.

An important step in maintaining a relationship is having closure with people. If past grudges, hurts, and disappointments have not been addressed, get them out in the open so healing can begin. Life is too short to hold onto past pain. At some point, it will be too late for regrets. What would have, could have, and should have been is not what is.

Matthew 18:15–17 says, "*If thy brother shall trespass against thee, go and tell him his fault between thee and him alone: if he shall hear thee, thou hast gained thy brother. But if he will not hear thee, then take with thee one or two more, that in the mouth of two or three witnesses every word may be established. And if he shall neglect to hear them, tell it unto the church: but if he neglect to hear the church, let him be unto thee as an heathen man and a publican.*"

Matthew 5:23-24 says, *"Therefore if thou bring thy gift to the altar, and there rememberest that thy brother hath ought against thee; Leave their thy gift before the altar, and go thy way; first be reconciled to thy brother, and then come and offer thy gift."*

The Bible puts ownership on *you!* Relationship closure leads to emotional freedom. If people don't know they hurt you, they have no way of making amends. How many of us have held onto past transgressions and seen it impact other relationships in a negative way? Meanwhile, the person causing so much emotional stress is living their life fancy free without the slightest idea of the torment in your life. God wants you to be free.

I will leave you with Matthew 7:2-5. It says, *"And why beholdest thou the mote that is in thy brother's eye, but considerest not the beam that is in thine own eye? Or how wilt thou say to thy brother, Let me pull out the mote out of thine eye; and, behold, a beam is in thine own eye? Thou hypocrite, first cast out the beam out of thine own eye; and then shalt thou see clearly to cast out the mote out of thy brother's eye."* None of us are perfect. Forgive, let go, and move on.

Celebrating the Deliverance from Sexual Shame

by Angela Davis

The sin and shame of sexual immorality is deeply rooted in emotional and spiritual pain. The source of this pain is Satan. This pain was conceived when I was raped at the age of nine. Sin incrementally grew into self-hatred, anger, bitterness, resentment, and envy.

As a young woman, I was not taught that premarital sex would taint my relationship with God, and I did not even feel ashamed. The examples of relationships with men from the women in my family showed me that women could do whatever they wanted. They thought the material possessions obtained by the men they were involved with would lead to emotional happiness. But those possessions represented empty promises. They masked their disappointments with drugs and alcohol. I understand now that the voids filled by earthly gain are cheap imitations for the true love of God. True joy could only be gained through the Love of God.

Through these revelations, I have acknowledged and accepted that I am a child of God and must act accordingly. I cannot live like the heathen. I used to have sex with men just because I wanted to. I was not mindful of the lasting spiritual consequences (though I did take natural precautions). I was not interested in commitment or marriage.

Men were just an end to justify a means. God gave us sexual desires, and I used them as I saw fit. By doing this, I was devaluing what He preciously created for His glory. If a man thought he had me, it was not so. I just used their male anatomy to serve my purpose. The fact that they were not men of character or integrity did not mean anything to me because I was not attached to them anyway.

When I did marry, there was no premarital counseling. I did not consider what a marital covenant meant in God's eyes. The root of sexual sin overshadowed every aspect of my life.

In the end, I was led to examine my own actions that resulted in my broken relationship with God. I love God more than anything. I love Him more than my fleshly desire for sexual pleasure, and I am mandated, out of my love for God, to sacrifice my wants. This sacrifice does not amount to a grain of sand compared to what Jesus sacrificed for us on the cross.

The rape I experienced at the age of nine forever changed my life in a way that only those who have been there can even begin to understand. My relationship with God is healing. I am excited to experience a pure fatherly love that I rarely experienced through the various father figures in my life as a child. I denounce, in the Name of Jesus, the shame of my body being used for unholy reasons. I denounce, in the Name of Jesus, self-unworthiness that hindered my ability to address this issue in the eyes of God. I pray it will help others expose the lie of the Devil and claim victory in their lives. I denounce, in the Name of Jesus, sexual immorality. I denounce, in the Name of Jesus, the mental, emotional, and spiritual conditioning that was formed in my heart and mind.

The rare examples of fatherly love led to a severe emotional, psychological, and spiritual drought. What happens when a plant has been parched by severe drought? Sometimes it survives with a need for special nurturing. The Bible says, *"A bruised reed shall he not break, and the smoking flax shall he not quench: he shall bring forth judgment unto truth"* (Isaiah 42:3).

He sent people in my life to confirm tangibly that He has me in His plans and view. Because I have been revived by the Holy Ghost, in the Name of Jesus, I claim peace. In the Name of Jesus, I claim worthiness. In the Name of Jesus, I claim love, joy, acceptance, and victory.

We are to be like little children in God's eyes. As I release my pain into His arms, I increase in understanding the depth of His love. I now see the beauty of what Fatherly love means.

Because I no longer have to view men through the lens of pain, I no longer harbor in my heart a barrier to the male aspect of spirituality, which speaks to Christ being the bridegroom and I being the bride. When I saw men, all I could think was how their anatomy could be used both for pleasure or as a weapon. This thought process hindered my ability to freely and honestly communicate with my heavenly father.

The special intimacy I desired and needed with God was tainted by the things I harbored in my heart. Men have a lot of weight and influence in a woman's life. There needs to be at least 10 positive experiences to overshadow the damage of one negative experience.

What does my sexual immorality and fatherly relationship have to do with my shame and God's love? It has plenty to do with it. Repentance is the beginning of Godly sorrow and deliverance. This in turn begins the releasing of guilt, shame, anger, and bitterness and the breaking of the demonic stronghold in my heart, mind, and soul.

This is not flowery nor is it something that most people want to talk about, but it must be exposed if I am determined to be free. Indeed I am determined.

I have made up in my mind and am convinced that my latter years will be greater than my former. I have found my keys to my new life in Christ. No one can take that away. No one can take the song from my heart and the spring in my spiritual steps. All this has taken place because of the Word of God. *"Not by might, nor by power, but by my spirit, saith the Lord of hosts."*

Do You Know?

by Ursula Lovely

Young man, do you know what a real man does?
That he is compassionate and is willing to show love.

Did you know that he is not full of self?
That he is helpful and will also know when to ask for help.

In times of trouble, he will care.
If he has little or much, he will share.

There are also times he will step up and be a dad,
Even though it's a child he has not had.

It's easy to say that you are a man and have all the right parts.
But the real man's actions will show and come from the heart.

He is not afraid to let you in or shoulder responsibility.
He will ask God for help and actually get on his knees.

Flights of Fancy

by LaTonja Brown

I have an extremely overactive imagination. God made me a writer, and it appears the gift comes with a side of drama and a very rich inner life.

An example of my over-the-top imagination occurred during a flight to Houston. The plane went through severe turbulence, and it occurred to my overactive imagination that this could be the end.

After accepting my fate, I prepared myself for the end. My fascination with Elizabeth I, England's Virgin Queen, led me to decide my last thoughts would be, "This is the Lord's doing; it is marvelous in our eyes."

Of course, I did not die, but the words led to more thinking. Whenever unpleasant situations happen in my life, I woefully decree, "*The Lord giveth, the Lord taketh away. Blessed is the Name of the Lord.*"

In truth, the decree has nothing to do with celebrating God's omniscient will over my life. It has more to do with me wallowing in self-pity. But what if my response to the good, the bad, and the ugly events in my life were, "This is the Lord's doing; it is marvelous in our eyes?" It would certainly change my reaction and brooding—I mean musing.

Second Corinthians 10:5 reads, "*Casting down imaginations, and every high thing that exalteth itself against the knowledge of God, and bringing into captivity every thought to the obedience of Christ.*"

This scripture is especially important when my desire takes my imagination in areas it should not be in my single state. In truth, in the past, I had a predictable schedule. Every two years for about six years, I would "succumb" to my temptation. Around year four, I recognized the pattern, and year six may have been a self-fulfilling prophecy.

Then, while reading Joseph's story, it hit me. Has God not been too good to me for me to do this sin against Him? This course of thought has helped me thus far in keeping myself, and it can be applied to all areas of my life.

The bottom line is we are bombarded with thoughts and desires that contradict with our faith. I find that it's human nature to jump to the worst-case scenario. Perhaps this is a coping mechanism. It also seems that we desire everything we cannot have. In fact, it seems we desire everything but what we have.

Regardless of our temptations and desires, God has been too good to us for us to sin against Him! Regardless of whether the devil "sent" the sin or your desire "conjured it up," God is faithful and just to keep you.

And he said, Thy name shall be called no more Jacob, but Israel:
for as a prince hast thou power with God and with men,
and hast prevailed.
—Genesis 32:28

IDENTITY AND CHOICE

What's in a Name?

by LaTonja Brown

I find irony in the following fact about the spelling of my first name. My mother named me LaTonia. The State of Mississippi named me LaTonla. The aunt who raised me named me LaTonja.

To go further, technically my last name is not Brown. My father's last name is Harris. Not only was I never given the right name, I was never told who I truly am. My name is technically LaTonia Harris, not LaTonja Brown. Yet I still continue to go by the wrong name. Is there any irony in that? No wonder I'm confused.

Why is there all this drama over a name?

We live in a society that tries to define us by our race, our gender, our occupation, or our economic status. The list of labels is exhaustive. The list has nothing to do with who we truly are, but people try to make it about our name.

I see red when I pass by a group of children and hear something along the following lines: "What's happening, nigga?" Or "Nigga, you should have seen it." I want to stop, shake them, and say, "Is his name nigga? Because if it is not, you are doing him a grave injustice to refer to him by something other than his given name."

But how do we put aside the wrong identities we have picked up over time? How do we become who we were born to be?

I had the most disconcerting experience recently. I realized that as I moved between groups of people, my ability to be free was compromised. How can I be seen in different ways in different groups? I had to ask myself how each group defined me. Is community defined by people who see you as you truly are and bring out the best of you in a healthy relationship?

I often want to ask people, "Do you see the real me?" The question is boldfaced, underlined, capitalized, and any other formatting I can use to help people hear the urgency of the question. I have been with people who I am not sure even really like me or approve of me. In fact, deep down, I know they don't. How can they accept me when they don't like or approve of me? It is the strangest experience to not feel safe in spaces that are supposed to be places of refuge. Is there a point when I stop celebrating peoples' lives that don't celebrate me?

The best example of seeking the wrong community is when my sister died over 10 years ago. The people I sought solace from were not people who truly cared for me. The sad thing is that I never sought solace from people who I knew were concerned about my welfare and mental state.

As we begin to understand ourselves better, what happens to those relationships that don't match who we are supposed to be? In other words, how does embracing who we are impact our current relationships?

Do we see people as they truly are and give them the freedom to be so? As we grow, do we seek places and groups that can fill the new wineskin? What if you feel like you are in places you shouldn't be or you have long outgrown comfortable relationships? But there is that comfort. That comfort often leads us to resurrect dead relationships in which the name you had is not the name you are striving to be.

My name is a feminine form of the Latin name Anthony. It is interpreted as meaning "worthy to be praised" or "beyond praise." I am not LaTonja the (mean) usher. I am not LaTonja, a single black woman. I will no longer adhere to the limits and constraints found in these labels. I will no longer be torn in two; I will live out who I am born to be (and I may need a little help in getting there).

Do not let where, what, or who you have been continue to define you. Let God redefine you. Enter a spring of your life as a young plant rooted firmly with its shafts finding their way to the surface. Step out of the shadow and live what you were born to be. Allow your name change to occur. Remember Jacob, the supplanter, became Israel; Abram became Abraham; Sarai became Sarah; Simon Barjona became Peter; Saul became Paul.

There is a moment of great revelation when you can freely say, *"Here am I; send me."*

Gone Backward

by Ursula Lovely

It seemed for awhile that Dr. King's dream had been fulfilled.
Now it shows the hidden side of our country and how it is still
    seriously ill.

It has shown us how sad the truth is that we are so unable
As men and women to come together and compromise and sit at
    the same table.

It seems as though the majority no longer wants to use God's plan
    and help those in need.
Instead, they want to benefit those who have been able to exploit
    themselves through greed.

It is our fault that we have not been more selective
And not watched the way that we have chosen our elected.

We've seen children on the news acting out the sins of their fathers
Going back in time again, treading troubled waters.

We need to reenter our churches and start again to gather
    and to pray.
We must stop relying on man and turn to God and ask Him to
    help us to make a better way.

Help Me

by Ursula Lovely

Help me, dear Lord, I pray,
To get through another day.
Help me to do this not as I would,
But please help me to do it as I should.

Judge Not

by Ursula Lovely

Help me, I pray, not to judge anyone.
How can I know where their faith comes from?
Only you know how they feel,
If what they do and say is for real.
Help me and guide me so that I know
That the things I do are out of love and not for show.

I Surrender

by Ursula Lovely

The hardest part of saving my soul is giving up my control.
I don't find it hard to give what little money I have as tender,
But saying, "Yes, Lord, you take the lead; I surrender."
I guess, as a black woman, my head is, oh, so hard.
I feel I know what is best and that I am so smart.
I know what I am doing is always right.
I fail to ask for deeper and wiser insight.
I jump in head first and with both feet,
And I don't understand why things I can't complete.
I know now that before I start a task,
I must look to God, give up control, and ask.

Dreams

by LaTonja Brown

I dream a lot. I daydream a lot as well.

There are recurring themes in the dreams. Buses—Missed Buses. Classes—Missed Classes. Forgotten Tests. Whales.

In my dreams, I search and long for something.

I am never where I should be. I should be in class or work, but I am wandering.

I am in class, but I forgot to study for a final.

I am running for a bus that pulls away right before I get there.

In the recent past, I dreamt I was pregnant. I remember that I did not want this baby, and I remember thinking, "I cannot and will not have this baby."

I then dreamt that I had an abortion. I went through a mourning process.

A week ago, I dreamt the abortion dream again. The dream was so heavy. When I woke up, I had to remind myself that it was a dream (This may have been part of the dream). I felt grief, guilt, and a heaviness that I couldn't shake.

I had questions about the dreams. Was God planting compassion in me to minister to women who have had abortions?

Was this God's way of telling me that I had let a gift or responsibility die?

I'm leaning toward the latter. I didn't want the baby. The baby would interfere with *my* life and *my* plans.

If I had recognized the blessing of the baby in my womb, I would have rejoiced at the wonder of the gift that was given.

The baby was not *my* baby. The baby was *our* baby.

There are so many talents, gifts, ideas, and compassions seeded in all of us. Will we cherish (want), cultivate, and birth these ideas? Or will the seeds go along the wayside and be choked out by life?

We are close to the harvest season. Fall is upon us, and it is time for the fruits of our labor to be reaped (birthed) for consumption and use during the winter that will follow.

A City Called Heaven

by Cheryl Boyd

I dreamed of a city called Heaven.
Its gates are opened wide.
And in that City of Heaven,
I walked in wonder inside.

There I saw the Lord was
Sitting alone
Up on a pure gold–laden throne.
He was saying to me with a smile,
"Come on in and look around, my child."

I dreamed of a city called Heaven,
Where pain and sickness
Are not there,
Where the blind see and the lame walk
And is void of all despair.

The grass is always healthy and green
And the sky is the prettiest
Blue I've ever seen.

I dreamed of a city called Heaven,
Where fighting—guns and weapons
Are laid down,
Where angels were dressed in glory
And pure white heavenly gowns.

With joy and peace in heart,
I know that I will
Never from my Savior depart.

I began to pray and thank Jesus
For such a place,
And I know some day
There's a house up there for me.

I dreamed of a city called Heaven.

God Said Live

by LaTonja Brown

In a prayer, Saint Francis of Assisi asked God to make him an instrument of peace. He desired to sow love where there was hate, pardon where there was injury, faith where there was doubt, hope where there was despair, light where there was darkness, and joy where there was sadness.

Ezekiel 16:6 reads, *"And when I passed by thee, and saw thee polluted in thine own blood, I said unto thee when thou wast in thy blood, Live; yea, I said unto thee when thou wast in thy blood, Live."* Despite God washing and caring for His people, they played the harlot. Even still, God remembered His covenant.

God kept His promise to Israel. Each time His people sinned, God was faithful and just to forgive them and keep His covenant. This covenant was sealed when Jesus Christ died on the Cross to pay for our sins and give us life. Because of Christ, no one is beyond repentance or forgiveness. No sin is too great that the Blood cannot cover it.

Before Jesus died on the Cross, He uttered the words, "It is finished." Christ completed His purpose, and His death gave us life. When Christ died on the Cross, He died for our sins, our hurts, our pains, and any—and everything else that attempts to hinder us. Christ replaced our death with life. He replaced our sin with redemption. He replaced our hurt and pain with healing.

Even if we stand polluted in our own sins, God is so faithful to forgive us. Even when we deserved the punishment of death, God's grace and mercy pardoned us. It is in this demonstration of the awesomeness of God's love for us that we can begin to become instruments of His peace.

Christ died that we could be light shining in the darkness. Christ died that we could be hope in the midst of despair. Christ died that we could be love in a world full of hate. Christ played His role; now we must play ours. Through Christ in us, we can sow and manifest the fruit of the Spirit.

Even in our darkest hour, deepest valley, and personal crisis, we can be comforted with the knowledge that our Lord and Savior, Jesus Christ, is with us. In Psalm 40, David said he waited patiently for God, and God heard his cry. David wrote of the Lord bringing him out of a horrible pit and out of the miry clay and placing his feet on solid rock and establishing his goings.

As we die out to ourselves, we are transformed into the likeness of Jesus Christ, who came that we could live.

Life or Death

by LaTonja Brown

As much as it pains me to confess this, I tend to flirt with danger and judge how close to the edge I can get without tumbling over. I am one of those people who like to dally with the slippery slopes Pastor talks about. Our poor Pastor has to deal with me dangling near the edge, occasionally. Pray for him! My most recent near escapade could have landed me in a heap of trouble, but I came to myself just in time.

These escapades normally deal with people and situations that God keeps telling me are finished. These are things that God kept me from even when I didn't want to be kept from them. The doors I try to reopen are full of unhealthy drama that could send me back at least ten years. The question is, how long will I linger and look back, like Lot's wife, on things or people God keeps telling me are not for me?

I am not even sure where some of my bright ideas come from. Things just occur to me from time to time. As James 1:4 says, "*But every man is tempted, when he is drawn away of his own lust, and enticed. Then when lust hath conceived, it bringeth forth sin: and sin, when it is finished, bringeth forth death.*"

The "it is finished" in James is a far cry from the "it is finished" uttered by Christ on the Cross. I choose to press toward the latter. When faced with the choice of life or death, I choose life.

My goal for this quarter is to heed Paul's words in Philippians 3:13-14. Paul wrote, "*Forgetting those things which are behind, and reaching forth unto those things which are before, I press toward the mark for the prize of the high calling of God in Christ Jesus."*

I don't really mind telling on myself, and I don't mind God's chastisement of me. I would rather be honest and end up doing the right thing than hide and continue to attempt to open doors that God has slammed shut.

I am glad that God has His Hand on me, and I am able to come to myself and recognize the behavior. If I leave the wrong doors closed, the right door will open for me, and I will be in a place to walk through it.

This theme is around completion and closure. In short, "It is finished." It is time for us to all realize what is truly finished and truly leave it behind us. There is no point in lingering and wondering about what could have been. It is time to stop wandering in the wilderness and move into our promise. "It is finished."

Redeeming the time, because the days are evil.
—Ephesians 5:16

TIME

An American Fairytale

by Ursula Lovely

Once upon a time, we had to work hard to obtain
Most major purchases or any major gain.
Along came the devil offering all pie in the sky.
He gave all the opportunity and not one questioned why.
People were trying to acquire in weeks things that usually
    took years.
Now it's time to pay up and all we have are tears.
The real villains of the story took their money and ran.
There are still scavengers trying to get all that they can.
When will we learn not to live so in greed,
That sometimes less is all that we need?
It's a shame we didn't seek God with the same enthusiasm.
We only seem to call on Him when we are falling in a deep
    chasm.
Hopefully the moral of the story, the lesson learned,
Is not to accept or go after things we have not earned,
To refuse to give into excessive greed,
That we use and seek not what we want but what we need.
Choose to always put God first; don't sit around waiting for
    disasters
And bubbles to burst.
Let Him be the captain of our team; believe me, life can be
    so much simpler
Than it seems.
Thank God, because through this I believe we will survive.
We have another chance. We can learn. We can serve, and with
    His help we
Will hopefully thrive.

Where Was God?

by Ursula Lovely

Where was God when I was almost raped as a child?
You said almost, think on that for a while.

Where was God when all I did was cry and asked repeatedly,
    "Why?"
God was there and gave you the strength to continue to try.

Where was God when my new husband was sent to Vietnam and
    with a newborn I was left alone?
God watched over him and brought him safely home.

Where was God when a young man broke into my house
    with a knife?
He allowed you to talk a mile a minute and saved your life.
He let you live on and continue to be a mother and wife.

Where was God when my mother, at the age of forty-six, died?
God was right there by your side.

Where was God when my child and I were held at gunpoint and
    robbed?
He let you live and gave you the sense to look for another job.

Where was God when my youngest son had a seizure and
    there was a code blue?
God was by your side at the hospital, and he did come back to you.

Where was God when I was young?
Why did he wait until I was old and gray?

God was there, but you refused to see or hear what it was that He
    had to say.

Through all of this where was God?
Because you finally got smart enough to try and understand and
    got the courage to ask and take a long, hard look at the past.

Where was God?
God is here, where He has always been, looking out for me
    from the beginning, and I pray that He will be here with me
    through the end.

Time to Begin Again

by Ursula Lovely

In the last nine years, we have seen horrors galore.
We have seen disastrous acts that have touched on our shores.

We sit around and act like there is nothing we can do.
But with prayer, change can come through me and you.

We aren't guaranteed a certain number of years in this place.
We need to heed God's Words because we don't have time to
    waste.

Do you realize we are on the brink of 2010?
A year that we can choose to continue our ways or to begin again.

God has given us this huge break.
He has looked down on us and said, "Listen and awake."

This is our chance to show God that we can change and start
    anew.
Take it and correct our ways and tell God Thank You.

Home Before the Dark

by Cheryl Boyd

Home before the dark
Is my hope and prayer.
Home before the dark
To wait do I dare?
"Home before the dark,"
He pleads; "Why hesitate?"
Home before the dark,
Don't let it be too late.
Home before the dark,
Where Jesus is waiting for me.
Home before the dark,
His precious face I'll see.
Home before the dark,
The sun is sinking fast.
Home before the dark,
Thank you, Jesus, home at last.

He sent his word, and healed them, and delivered them
from their destructions.
—Psalm 107:20

HOPE

A Miracle in Haiti

by Ursula Lovely

Did you see in the news the sixteen-month-old girl
    they found alive?
What helped this baby alone in that dark place want to survive?
How did she hang on under all that rubble,
Without parents, food, and water for days in all this trouble?
They moved a rock, and she saw a light and walked out.
I wonder if we would see the light.
I guess that's what God's miracle is all about.

Yours to Give

by Ursula Lovely

Have you ever seen how adoringly a baby looks at you?
Did you ever wonder in order to keep that look what you
　　had to do?

It doesn't take much,
A little affirmation by word or touch.

It works on adults as well as a child,
A hug, a kiss, or an encouraging smile.

It won't take a lot and it's yours to give.
The kindness and warmth, that feeling of love that makes you
　　want to live.

You don't need a lot of money or the things you buy.
Just get up tomorrow, make up your mind, and give it a try.

Yes, You're the One!

by Cheryl Boyd

Am I the one?
Did you shed your blood for me?
Am I the one,
Why you died on Calvary?
Am I the one
Who was saved from sin and
Was set free?
Tell me, Jesus; tell me, Lord.
Am I the one?

"Yes, you're the one."
This I heard my Savior say.
"Yes, you're the one;
Take my hands as I pass by.
Yes, you're the one;
I was nailed on the cross for you.
Yes, you're the one;
I will ever be so true.
Yes, you're the one!"

Am I the one?
Did you do it all for me?
"Yes, you're the one,
Why I died upon a tree."
Am I the one

Why He suffered on the cross?
"Yes, you're the one,
And I counted it but loss."
Am I the one?
"Yes, you're the one!"

Yes, you're the one!

Motherhood

by Angela Davis

People often asked me how many children I have. I would reply, depending on the circumstances, with glee or frustration that I have three children.

The consistent reply would be, "Wow, you really have your hands full."

That was not the complete story. I had my hands full—full of laundry, dishes, bills, or Kleenex.

I also had my brain way too full preparing for developmental changes.

My eyes were roaming everywhere in the hopes of warding off any potential traumatic events that would end up on someone's counseling couch.

And, finally, my eyes were examining everyone so that my cubs would survive in this world.

I must tell you that motherhood is a job that is never boring, and you will never hear a mother complain about any lack of challenges.

To share a true message of motherhood, I would say my heart is full. It is full of love, sadness, joy, heartache, and laughter. But, most of all, my heart is full of the anticipation of seeing what these precious little people will become. And then I will know that my work was well done.

Songs of Sadness

by LaTonja Brown

I do not know
Why
You come to me
With songs of sadness.
You tell me,
"Listen to the rain
Gently falling;
They are your soul
Crying."

I do not know
Why
You come to me
With songs of joy.
You tell me,
"Listen to the wind
Blowing through trees;
It is you
Singing to me."

I do not know
Why
You come to me,
But you come.

In my nightmares of yesterday,
In my dreams of today,
In my daydreams of tomorrow,

You come
To me.

Harlem's Song

by LaTonja Brown

When I scream
With a loud voice,
It is then,
And only then,
That you hear me.
I wish I could
Speak softly
To you.
I would watch
The sunset
With you.
I would tell you
I long to be
With you
Seconds before
Midnight
So you could tell me
We could make it
Into day.
We would wake
To the sunrise, and
We would start
Our time
Together.

Contributors

Cheryl M. Harding Boyd moved to the Seattle area in 1976 from Calgary, Alberta, Canada. She came from a family of ten whose grandparents migrated from Missouri and Oklahoma to Canada. She was married to Trustee Larry Boyd for thirty-three years, and they had one son, Lawrence Jr. She started writing poetry in her early twenties, at the lowest point of her life, to express the pain she was going through. She continued writing after that. Her first poem was "Thank you Jesus, Thank you Lord." She wrote it while she sat on the banks of a river in Canada.

After moving to Seattle, she became very active in the church. She was an usher, greeter, and Sunday-school teacher. She also worked with the Women's Auxiliary and was in the choir. God gifted her with the gift of discernment and visions, which inspired her poetry. She was a powerful prayer warrior and intercessor who loved to spend hours laboring before the Lord for the souls He laid on her heart.

She was grateful to her pastor and first lady for their encouragement and for their empowering her to step out in her gifts and calling. Even when stricken with MS, she continued to minister in intercessory prayer, hold onto God, and be a spiritual encouragement to others.

LaTonja Brown has been writing since she was a young child. She used to sit on a curb outside of her house and think about her future. She can remember writing poems when she was in elementary school while sitting on that curb.

In elementary, junior high, and high school, she can remember spending many lunch hours in the library, poring over books and getting lost in the magic of the tales the writers had woven. In short, she has always loved words.

Because of this love, she studied English with a writing emphasis, focusing on poetry and expository writing, at the University of Washington, where she received a bachelor of arts degree. She has a certificate in commercial fiction writing and a certificate in editing from the University of Washington.

For the past twelve years, she has been an editor and writer for the *PCC Women's Scroll/PCC Scroll*. She is a staff writer and associate editor for the *Compass Point* monthly e-newsletter published by the Port of Seattle's Commercial Strategy department. Prior to that, she wrote for and associate-edited other Port of Seattle newsletters, including *T.E. You!* and *Transport*. She has co-written for the *Tacoma Daily Index* and edited for the quarterly Women Transportation Seminar newsletter.

In addition, she has written and published for anthologies published at Grace Apostolic Temple (*Gentle Explosion of Words*) and at Pentecostal Covenant Church (*Who We Are* and *Scribbler*).

You can follow her blog at http://latonja.blogspot.com.

Angela Davis began writing for creative expression when she was a teenager. As she began to share her writings, she continually received positive feedback. She was often asked what she was going to do with her work.

As she matured, she became intrigued with how news broadcasters mastered how to say a whole lot without saying anything at all. This led her on a quest of learning about the fundamentals of communication. If one could say a whole lot with nothing, then saying very little with substance would be that much more powerful.

Angela received a bachelor of arts in communications in 2007 from Seattle University. She has had a few of her writings published in the *PCC Scroll*.

I asked Angela about her writing goals. This is how she answered:

"My goal is to earn a living doing what I love. I want to be a vessel for the Lord through the power of the pen as God inspires me to do so."

Ursula Lovely is a sixty-nine-year-old wife and the mother of four children (two boys and two girls). She has five granddaughters ranging in age from twenty-two to three years old.

She was born in Gary, Indiana, in 1944 to two geniuses. Her mother graduated from high school at the age of sixteen, and her father was valedictorian of his class. When she was young, Ursula loved music and art. But she was not allowed to "waste her time." She attended private schools and studied Latin, and to this day, she can't remember one word of it. She attended Indiana University, Gary extension, where she met and fell in love with her husband of forty-nine years, Carl.

Her mother passed away at the age of forty-six, and that prompted her first attempt at writing a poem. She attempted one a year after that for special occasions.

We asked her what inspired her to write poetry. And the following is her answer:

"As I look back, my poetry comes from some deep hurts. But I feel that God has infused them with hope and the knowledge that He has been and will always be there. Some of them come from things that are happening around us every day: the weather, wars, elections, and even children at play. I never intend for the words to rhyme, but that seems to happen all the time. I feel things deep down inside. God is always on my mind, and it feels like He takes over quite a lot of the time. I get a thought and the words come. I begin to write and get lost in thought and don't stop until I am through. It's like being in a trance or being led in a dance, and you can't stop until the music is through."

Zarriah Polk would like to be a fashion designer when she grows up. She enjoys reading, drawing, and playing with makeup. She also enjoys spending time with her family playing games, eating, and talking. She likes to play outside and go on walks with her parents and brother. She is inspired to write when she is in quiet, peaceful places. She desires to have three books published.

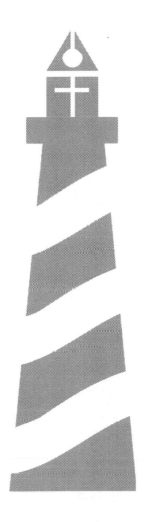

About Pentecostal
Covenant Church

Pentecostal Covenant Church

Pentecostal Covenant Church was founded in June 1995 by Pastor Wilford T. and Minister Jo Ann Hairston. Both are trained facilitators who believe in team ministry and have a love for God and God's people. They often facilitate relationship and marriage seminars. They have the philosophy and theme "Empowered by God to Empower Others."

Mission

To reach the unbeliever with the love of Christ and the Good News of the Gospel and to empower believers to live a fully-committed life in Christ. To influence the youth in our church and community and support and strengthen the family unit.

Statement of Purpose

To bring people to Christ and membership into the body of believers (God's family) and develop them to Christ-like maturity and equip them for ministry in the church and community in order to fulfill their destiny and magnify Jesus Christ.

Purpose Elements

To love the Lord with all your heart—through Worship.

—Matthew 4:19; Psalm 34:3

To love your neighbor as yourself—through Ministry.

—Ephesians 4:12

To go and make disciples—through Evangelism.

—Matthew 28:19-20;
Mark 16:15; Luke 24:47-49;
John 20:21; Acts 1:18

We are to baptize them—into Fellowship.

—Matthew 28:19-20; Ephesians 2:19

We are to teach them to obey God's Word—through Discipleship.

—Colossians 1:28; Ephesians 4:12-13;
John 17; Acts 2:1-47

We are to inspire them to be Spirit-filled believers—through Teaching.

—Acts 1:8; Acts 2

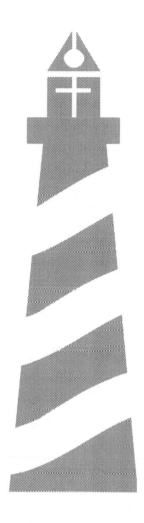

Credits

Brown: "Dreams" originally published July 1, 2007, volume VI, issue III of *PCC Women's Scroll*

Brown: "Flights of Fancy" originally published July 1, 2008, volume VII, issue III of *PCC Women's Scroll*

Brown: "God Said Live" originally published April 1, 2010, volume IX, issue II of *PCC Scroll*

Brown: "God Will Perfect It" originally published July 1, 2011, volume X, issue III of *PCC Scroll*

Brown: "The Last Debate" originally published January 1, 2007, volume VI, issue I of *PCC Women's Scroll*

Brown: "Life or Death" originally published October 1, 2010, volume IX, issue IV of *PCC Scroll*

Brown: "Reflections of India" originally published October 1, 2006, volume V, issue IV of *PCC Women's Scroll*

Brown: "Relationship Freedom" originally published July 1, 2010, volume IX, issue III of *PCC Scroll*

Brown: "Spiritual Healing" originally published January 1, 2009, volume VIII, issue I of *PCC Women's Scroll*

Brown: "Spiritual Remodel" originally published October 1, 2008, volume VII, issue IV of *PCC Women's Scroll*

Brown: "What's in a Name" originally published April 1, 2007, volume VI, issue II of *PCC Women's Scroll*

Lovely: "Gone Backward" originally published October 1, 2011, volume X, issue IV of *PCC Scroll*

Lovely: "In Sixty Seconds" originally published July 1, 2011, volume X, issue III of *PCC Scroll*

Lovely: "Kaida: A Story of Puppy Love" drawings

Lovely: "Where Was God?" originally published July 1, 2012, volume XI, issue III of *PCC Scroll*

Polk: "The Prince and the Fairy Princess" drawing